Reflections

of a Young Man

by

Hayden Skaggs

Sit down to eat more. Speak less. Love blindly. Move daily. Act with kindness. React with ruthlessness. Give no quarter, and accept none in return. Forgive those who slight you, but never forget it. Waste no time; yours or that of others. Don't be in a rush. Hurry up and execute. Most of all; seek out that which gives you purpose. You will find purpose in the search itself.

Do not shield yourself from that which is hard and harsh in this life. Seek out the things that uplift you and make you love your position in this world. But, shy not from the things that demand trial and hardships. Those tests will manifest within you a gratitude for tranquility, peace, and light-heartedness. Experiencing what is accepted as "bad" in this life will foster a genuine appreciation for the "good".

Living life with an expectation of a constant euphoric existence sets one up for massive fallout when even the slightest of slights should happen upon the path. However, you are obligated to not only weather, but embrace and triumph over the travesties of this short journey. When you can endure these things to come out stronger and with a hearty laugh at the survivability of it all, you armor yourself against life's injustices. You then become impervious; uninjurable by the many spears of this being.

To be alive is to be an agent of change. To have the ability to change is the surest sign of life. So long as you are able to change, be it yourself or your environment, you have some semblance of control. This control is best exhibited over your own temperament. If you control how you endure your hardships, you have won life's greatest battle. That when something happens which would defeat a lesser man, it is but a cool breeze to the likes of you. You are no Ubermensch, but also no caitiff; unplagued by the degradation of men.

Take then the strength you have learned, and teach it to your sons. Let them teach it to their sons after them. But, do not stop at them. Preach not to the masses, but give of yourself to every worthy man and woman you meet. Show them there is a way. Bring them out into the morning sun, and let them bask in the power of inoculation.

You needn't lecture nor cavil of their ways. You only need to do. They will see the manner in which you captain yourself, and will choose one of many ways. Some will cast hate and jealousy; their demeanor should have no sway on your path, as they are merely observers. Others will remain indifferent, unswayed themselves. And yet, the fewest of them will draw strength from you. They will hope to keep up or surpass you. Let them try. If they do, be happy for your fellow man, for they may spread the fire you have started. And if you cannot hold joy for him, then there is only to push your own self further, to usurp he who would best you. Unspoken competition drives the world forward.

Sit down to eat more.

When you go to have a meal, especially with others, have a seat; preferably around a large table, with more than enough room for all to join. Make merry over the foods you are consuming. This is a time to celebrate, pontificate, and give thanks for this adventurous life.

Do not bring bleakness to the table, as it is unfit for the air of gratitude that should accompany the provision of sustenance. If the food at your front is more than that which merely waylays your death, then there is much to be thankful for; even then, continuity itself is sufficient for change. And if you have someone with which to share your meal, all the better. Their presence is good tiding.

More has been learned and exchanged by way of food than by the pen and the press. Let not the burdens of your days infringe upon your countenance. All that is at the table should be your present world. Nothing matters else but the shared experience and feelings from the table's proceedings.

Look your counterparts in the eye. Connect with them, and invest in their musings; truly. Seek to understand their words and intentions. If you cannot find merit or validity in what they say, then find their *why*. Their *why* will give insight to much more than the surface of what is merely said. Hope, but don't expect, that they do so in kind. At a minimum, you have learned more about an adversarial viewpoint, and can therefore better articulate, (and by extension validate), your position against it.

Most of all, etch this time into your soul as part of that which is good. Every *good* can be used as a link in your mail.

Speak less.

To verbalize too often is a selfish want to be heard. To listen is the selfless act of hearing. Every moment you spend speaking is another moment you spend not learning. Can you teach others of the knowledge you have gained? Of course. However, you could speak for every waking second of the rest of your life, and teach the masses from only your point of view. Or, you could be silent for the same, and learn the world from them all.

Observe. Truly digest what you see and hear. When you take in new information, do not accept its face value. Dig deeper and find the why. In this pursuit, you will find no end. Good. There will always be more to do. The less you say, the more you are able to receive. The more you receive, the more you realize how much you have yet to receive. Say naught but your questions, and you may gain more than your lot.

There will come times for you to be heard, but they will be far scarcer than the times in which you need to do the hearing. If you spend your adolescence and emerging adulthood in the fashion of constant declaration, how can you possibly absorb enough along the way to give your sons wisdom when they need it later in life? They will look to you in the moments when their knowledge falls short. If you have not been receptive during those moments in your own life, and they will be many, you will not be sufficiently equipped to aid them. That is a ramification you cannot accept.

Furthermore, there will be moments unforeseen in which others, both close and unfamiliar, will need the guidance you provide. They will need parts of you that you didn't know you had. You will have gained what you must give them by being customarily receptive. Think of how many times you alone have needed such counsel, and how much you will need it yet. Quiet yourself, so that perhaps you can spare few from the troubles of many.

Love blindly.

Man is not as advanced as he would care to believe. He is oft no greater than his mammalian, reptilian, and amphibian counterparts. But, in a few sterling moments, he ascends his primordial self, and shines with an effervescent uniqueness. He builds megalithic structures, cures illnesses, and even keeps other men and other beasts at his bay. However, in no greater moment does man display his absolute humanity than in that of love.

Love is a largely displaced variable that has gone previously unaccounted for in this Great Being. Love is illogical. It does not make proof of the natural laws that govern our physical and metaphysical being. Love, in all forms, is to put someone or something before the self. That one may eat when you are starving. That you may accept the spear, so another is spared. Very few people experience true love to a heightened degree, because they are afraid of harm. Protecting yourself by being unwilling to give all of yourself to someone or something is the surest sign of cowardice.

Your armor has built through callous and scar; hardened into a steely imperviousness. Will you wear this armor for all your days? When you lay down to bed with your queen? What will your sons think of the armor you wear? Never revealing your face beneath the helmet of war.

You can and must protect yourself from the masses, if you have any hope for continuity and wisdom. But you needn't be so warlike when you are sitting face-to-face with one of these earthly divinities. In peering through their windows, you will often find one as naked and as vulnerable as you.

Even the nude can conceal a blade; cutting you deeper than you knew a blade could go. And yet you are alive. You may be wounded, you may be on your knees. But you are not ended. Go, heal. Mend yourself. Notch a tally in your armor. It is one of many you will inscribe. But do not think your armor so impenetrable, that you cannot be harmed. For, though you may be spared the stave, regret shall lay hold of you in the end. Do not shy away from that which makes you most human.

To love without hindrance is the greatest supposition of selflessness. And that which is selfless surely could be deemed as *good*; of which there is too little in this world. Take stock of what you are giving, and give a little more without reservation or affectation.

Move daily.

The purpose of man is not to sit idle at rest. Man is supposed to trek across continents, build grand edifices, create technological marvels, and fight with weapons of war. Man is, by design, incredibly capable of staying in perpetual motion. And thus should he stay, lest he fall into tarnish and age. Machines that continually move will only be worn by wear itself, but surely they will not rust.

A hardened body is a sure sign of a hardened mind. The discipline required to be adequately capable of fighting, trekking, and building is found only in the hearts of men whom would see their will be done. The lazy, impotent, and caitiffs of this world cower at any sign of pain. Pain is requisite for building strength. You will be sore. You will be tired. But you will be able to press on.

Through physical test, you may continually further your mental limits. Therefore, hardening the body will also harden the mind. Deftly utilizing the two in concert is the heartiest achievement of man. For, when you can conceptualize a thing, then work physically to make it come to fruition, you will love that thing. And anything done through love can most times be deemed a good thing.

Act with kindness.

The act of giving is one so seldom witnessed in nature. The leaf does not give itself to the stag. Nor does the antelope lend himself to the lion. These, and things numerous elsewise, are taken. To take is standard. It is natural and can be deemed neither good nor bad; that, being decided only by circumstance.

But, all taking can be deemed selfish. Selfish is the logical way of things. High states flow to low states because low states are at want. The Great Being works all in this manner.

We humans are largely illogical. We love when we should hate. We hate when we should love. But sometimes, we give when we should take. This giving is scarcely found, though it might be supposed commonplace. When you give, no matter what the giving be, you are shedding yourself of something you could have otherwise used. Food, accoutrements, energy, and time. The last of those being that which you can never take back.

This is illogically selfless. Why give when you could take? Because perhaps, you may cause some small bit of good in this world; even if momentarily. These moments add up to memories of that which to be thankful for at the end of one's life. You may not remember extending your hand to ten different men. But, ten different men will remember the exact moment in which you extended your hand.

React with ruthlessness.

The caitiff will tell you that there is power in forgiveness. The coward will tell you the same. It is far easier to forgive than to retaliate. But, consider that the King may say so too.

Power itself resides in the ability to control. Nowhere will you have more power than when you exhibit control over yourself. You may truly decide how you react to any and all slights that happen to you. In that, there is the utmost of power.

When you are given the choice of retaliation or forgiveness, pick whatever you deem best, and pursue the course of action with the conviction of a man who knows he is going to die. If you forgive, be ruthless only with yourself; discipline yourself so that the forgiveness is thorough and complete. Exchange gifts, and lay your quarrels to rest. If you retaliate, speak not of its doing; strike from a shadow, and bury your enemy completely. Time it may take, but you cannot stop until the task is complete. A crippled enemy may strike back the hardest. You must be completely and utterly relentless. They assuredly will be.

Give no quarter, and accept none in return.

You have no duty nor moral obligation to have mercy. Moral obligations are for those tethered to another's code. You are bound only to yourself, and those you love. Even they cannot decide if you are a good man. Only you must live with the reality of your actions; and they needn't be merciful. Most often, they cannot be.

If you choose clemency, so be it. But, choose it not out of convenience; only from conviction that it is what is best for you, given circumstance. Most others will not choose to be so lenient if they would act upon you in the same manner. They will grant you no pardon. And if they do, should you accept? Who are you to not lay claim to the ramifications of your actions? Your outcome is your own. No other is obliged to bear it for you. Therefore, accept no pardon. And do not be quick to grant it in return. Many of the greatest lessons in this Great Being occur in the aftermath of our transgressions.

It is far better to learn from others' mistakes. But, none will bite as deep as your own. Take yoke and reign as one. Sow the seed of redemption, and tend your field over time. Soon will blossom the flowers of restored honor. It is an undertaking most hearty, but most worthy. So, if you may be willing to return your name to good standing as such, should you then hold others to a lower standard? Should they be exempt from the labors of rejuvenation? That will be decided in tempo.

Should you choose to steadfastness, you mustn't relent. Your transgressors will be forced to shoulder their own Great Burden. Or break. Your precedent is set. If you fail in being stalwart after already demanding retribution, you are surely a coward. Exact your punishment, and be swift in its discharge. No one will respect the man who draws out his actions to unruly or unscrupulous means. Nor will they respect the man who speaks but does not act.

Softness from the hardened man means more than hardness from the man who is soft.

Forgive those who slight you, but never forget it.

You cannot hope to surmount every affront by way of force and cunning. In some cases, there is only to absolve our debtors. You will know when the time to do so is right. It may be by cause of goodness, morality, or strategy. The means matter not. All which matters is that the tally be recanted. Though hurt may never be reversed, *harm* can never truly befall the man who forgives. But, only if he may pardon for the right reasons.

He who pardons is exempt from the mental cacophony of hatred. It is space, time, and energy given to a cause in which the seeing through can never restore the resources spent. Much simpler it is to grant clemency.

If you are to grant absolution, reserve instead a space for the deed of he who you have absolved. Though the deed may harm you not, you have learned of the nature of your offender. To know the nature of those who may slight you is the surest way to prevent a slight. The course of forgiveness is not implicit of rewelcoming with open arms; merely the extinguishment of a previous wrong. Should you decide to embrace your wrongdoer, keep a blade tucked in your belt. It is the nature of snakes to bite.

Waste no time; yours or that of others.

Your stay will not last. You will walk through That Door, never to return. But, dwell not upon what is in the Next Room. Your present enclave is all that need concern you until the moment Else is revealed. Pontification is never a foolhearted endeavor. However, seldom will be your moments of rest when there is provided time to contemplate beyond the reaches of this Great Being.

Most of your days will be spent in labor of life and love. Good. This means you are *alive*. Too many are merely living. In your ventures, you will do things both for the self, and for those aside. In neither should you be wont to tarry. You may eat when you are starving, and will regain your strength. You may lose your lot of worldly things, and win them back in stride. But you cannot grow old and hope to again feel your youth.

How could you possibly sit idle? How could you possibly watch as the world happens around you? What will you tell your sons? That you were merely present *when*? Or, will you tell them that you *did*? That you acted when it was your turn to act. Do not be the Old Man who sits without wisdom and the stories that created it. Fewer than you know will get the privilege to be the Old Man.

If your time is precious and not to be wasted, surely the same respect should be extended to others. They don't have a life. They are a life. Commit to be an actor in their happening, or take leave. To squander another's days is amongst the surest of slights; a theft forever unsettled.

You cannot go back. You cannot stand still. Make your charge headlong towards The Door. Intend for your death to be well-deserved.

Don't be in a rush. Hurry up and execute.

Time is not given, nor is it taken. You are merely here to perceive it; to experience the moment you are in. The happenings of this life are not up to you. Your temperament is, however, most under your control. Guide it towards thinking, feeling, and experiencing all that which resides in the present. Nothing else exists. Nothing else matters. Because nothing matters but by way of perspective. Your perspective is you. And you may only perceive in the *here* and the *now*.

Pause to savor the caress of the woman you love. Breathe deep of the air in the mountains. Attend to the sound of the winds through the trees. The sight of your sons as they first open their eyes will be that which lasts you your lifetime. You cannot rush those days. Yet those days will rush to leave you. And you will cling to them until you expire.

Idleness is the surest sign of death. You must make do of that which is your lot. For, the only Grand Purpose is transpiration itself. Should you sit and wait for it to come hither, you will pass through That Door wanting of substance. The time for doing is now. Relish in it.

Most of all; seek out that which gives you purpose. You will find purpose in the search itself.

Man confuses happiness with fulfillment. Life was never designed to be happy. It was designed to be trying and harsh. The moments of happiness that are interspersed in this Great Being give cause for striving. What man truly seeks is fulfillment. But, what can man fulfill if he has no purpose?

Man seeks out meaning in everything he contrives. The most of which could assuredly be his own life. He wants to know that he played his role, and that he played it well. Playing it well would be fulfillment. But finding his role is that from which derives purpose. If he meanders through life not achieving or committing himself to any good cause, then he is without purpose, and therefore cannot be fulfilled.

Some men find purpose in raising children. Others, in raising empires. You will be the only man that can truly decide what will bring you purpose. Someday you will stand with your hand on That Door, ready to enter the Next Room. Will you have let others dictate whether or not what you have done has had meaning? You cannot. Therefore, you must only be and do that in which you have found meaning.

Purpose will not find you. It will not approach you in the shadows of your mind, hoping to draw you in. Purpose is a decision. *You* must find *it*. If you have no purpose today, you may find it tomorrow. But, you will only find it if you are willing to do and be. What though? Anything and everything.

This life is short enough for urgency, yet long enough for experience. Try a new thing today. And another tomorrow. You will find something that sets you ablaze. If not this day, perhaps the next. Once you find it, do not stop searching for that which is new and unfamiliar to you. Man may have more than one purpose in this life.

When you get there, the Doorman beckoning you through, you will realize that your purpose may have been a thing, or it may have been many things; but mostly, you will find that your purpose was everything. Each deed you had done, each action you had taken, amounted to a life full of meaning. This is especially true, if you have endeavored to be selfless.

Though it would seem that these actions may not matter in the grand scheme of things, remember this: it meant something to someone, somewhere, for even an iota of time. Therefore, it mattered.

Jeg er Vildhjärta.

Jeg vil glemme ikke det.

Made in the USA
Middletown, DE
31 October 2023

41679425R00022